EQUALITY IN
AMERICAN SCHOOLS

by Lillian Forman

PEARSON

Scott
Foresman

Editorial Offices: Glenview, Illinois • Parsippany, New Jersey • New York, New York
Sales Offices: Needham, Massachusetts • Duluth, Georgia • Glenview, Illinois
Coppell, Texas • Ontario, California • Mesa, Arizona

ISBN: 0-328-13429-5

8 9 10 V0G1 14 13 12 11 10 09 08

Before the 1950s the laws of some states forced African Americans to use different facilities from those that white Americans used. They had to drink from separate water fountains, eat in separate restaurants, go to separate hospitals, and learn in separate schools.

In 1868 the Fourteenth Amendment to the Constitution of the United States officially recognized that African Americans, recently freed from slavery, were citizens. It gave them all the rights of citizens, including "equal protection under the law." The Fifteenth Amendment, passed in 1870, made it illegal for anyone to prevent a citizen from voting because of race.

Segregated movie theater

There were many acts of **discrimination** against African Americans. After the Civil War ended on April 26, 1865, the U.S. government sent soldiers to the South. They were there to protect African Americans and to make sure that no one prevented them from voting. During this period, called Reconstruction, many African Americans became leaders in their state governments and representatives in the U.S. Congress.

Reconstruction ended in 1877, and the federal troops withdrew. This left African Americans unprotected. Many white Southerners wanted African Americans to live in separate communities. They kept African Americans from voting. As a result, after Reconstruction, people who had supported the Confederacy still governed the South. These legislators wanted to keep African American and white people separate. They turned such practices into laws.

Soldiers of different ethnic backgrounds at a camp in Pennsylvania

5

1896 · Separate but Equal

In the late 1800s the Supreme Court said that segregation of African Americans and white people was in agreement with the Constitution, as long as they were separate but equal. The places for African Americans had to be equal to those for white people.

Did this really mean that African Americans had the same rights as white people? Suppose you find out that a group of students has taken over a table in the cafeteria. When you try to sit there, the group tells you to go somewhere else even if there is room. They point out that the other tables are the same. As a result you feel that the members of the group think that they are better than you and do not want you around.

Separate but Equal?

Do you think the students in these pictures have equal opportunities?

The **doctrine** of "separate but equal" does not make segregation right. Political leaders of the late 1800s failed to provide equal facilities for African Americans. Little money was spent on African American facilities. African American schools, for example, were not as good as those used by white people.

Perhaps the most important public facility is school. It is in school that people learn about citizenship and prepare themselves for the future. It is in school that people learn about their own culture as well as other people's cultures. A poor school leaves its students at a disadvantage.

James Weldon Johnson

In the mid-1920s African Americans in a group called the National Association for the Advancement of Colored People (NAACP) decided to do something about this inequality. James Weldon Johnson, a poet, led the group in a series of lawsuits to force school boards to spend as much money on African American schools as they did on white schools.

These lawsuits were also meant to start **integration,** or the inclusion of people of all racial backgrounds in public places. The NAACP planned to do this in three ways:

- by advertising to the American public how African Americans were discriminated against

- by showing African Americans that they could fight against inequality

- by making it so expensive to provide "separate but equal" facilities that white Southern taxpayers would accept the idea of integration

The NAACP was not able to carry out this plan at the time. They needed more money and more African American lawyers to do so. Fortunately, in the 1930s, a group of African American leaders took up the challenge.

One of these leaders was a lawyer named Thurgood Marshall. He worked with another African American lawyer, Charles Hamilton Houston, to fight segregation in public schools. At first Marshall and Houston tried to win equal conditions for African American graduate students, or people continuing their studies after college. They felt that white judges would respect the achievements of these young people.

Marshall and Houston went on to win many cases. Two of the most important victories were in the late 1940s. They both involved **aspiring** lawyers—Herman Sweatt and George McLaurin.

Herman Sweatt applied to the University of Texas School of Law and was rejected. True to the doctrine of separate but equal, the state of Texas gave the university money to build a law school for African Americans. Until the new school was built, however, Sweatt had to attend a makeshift school in the basement of a building. When the new school was built, it was not as good as the University of Texas School of Law.

Thurgood Marshall

George McLaurin applied to the University of Oklahoma. Since Oklahoma had no law school for African Americans, the university had to accept McLaurin as a student. He sat in the same classroom as white students, but he sat alone.

In 1950 Marshall brought these cases to the Supreme Court and won. In Sweatt's case, the Supreme Court justices agreed that the facility for African American students was not equal to the one for white students. In McLaurin's case, they recognized that sitting alone prevented him from participating in class.

The Supreme Court ruled that Sweatt and McLaurin should be treated the same as other students. However, separate but equal facilities were still allowed in other places.

George McLaurin is forced to sit alone in a classroom of white students.

These Supreme Court rulings gave Marshall a way to fight segregation in elementary and high schools. The rulings proved that McLaurin's isolation within the classroom had made his education inferior. Marshall hoped that this would make it easier for the NAACP to show that all forms of segregation were harmful.

Many parents asked their local NAACP to help them get better school conditions for their children. Some parents just wanted their segregated schools to be as good as the white schools. Marshall and other NAACP leaders persuaded these people to demand that their children be admitted to white schools.

Oliver Brown of Topeka, Kansas, did not want his nine-year-old daughter, Linda, to have to cross train tracks and a busy street to get to her bus stop. At first he wanted safer transportation for her, but then he realized that the white school was only a few blocks away. It made more sense to ask that Linda be allowed to attend that school.

Linda Brown's case was first tried in the U.S. District Court for the district of Kansas in 1951. This court agreed that segregation made African American children feel less valued. However, Linda Brown still was not allowed to go to school with the white students.

Linda Brown, as a child (above)

Cheryl Brown Henderson, Linda's sister, speaking at a celebration fifty years after the _Brown_ v. _Board of Education_ decision, along with President George W. Bush (left)

In 1952 Thurgood Marshall brought Brown's case before the Supreme Court. The Court did not make a decision at that time. The case was opened again in 1953 and was argued using the Fourteenth Amendment, which gives all citizens, of any ethnic background, equal rights and equal protection under the law. In 1954 Chief Justice Earl Warren read the Court's unanimous, or fully agreed upon, decision in favor of Linda Brown. The Court concluded that separate schools are unequal. It also stated that anyone forced to go to a segregated school is "deprived of the equal protection of the laws guaranteed by the Fourteenth Amendment."

This landmark decision was a great victory for African Americans, but it was just the beginning of a long and difficult struggle. The Supreme Court justices knew that many white people would fight against allowing African American children into their schools. They decided that integration should take place in a slow but steady manner.

Southern politicians found three ways to fight the *Brown* v. *Board of Education* decision. One of these **tactics** was to do nothing about helping integration along. Another was to refuse to obey the laws against segregation. The third involved violence. Mobs of people threatened and insulted African American students who tried to attend white schools.

Shortly after the Supreme Court had declared school segregation unconstitutional, a group of people in Mississippi formed the White Citizens Council to fight integration. The members of the White Citizens Council and similar groups took legal and illegal measures to prevent African American children from entering white schools. Besides handing out leaflets to advertise their own point of view, they hurt those who did not agree with them. The members boycotted, or refused to buy from, businesses whose owners did not support segregation. They fired African American employees who tried to insist on the rights of their children.

The people who were against integration became more active. Newspapers showed photographs of mobs **jeering** at African American students, who only wanted an equal education.

Instead of being discouraged, African Americans continued to fight. New laws were made, ending segregation in all public facilities. In 1967 Thurgood Marshall became the first African American U.S. Supreme Court justice.

Integration did not progress quickly, though. In 2004, on the fiftieth anniversary of the *Brown v. Board of Education* decision, educators met at Central Missouri State University. They found that schools were becoming segregated again, partly because our nation had not been paying attention to desegregation. The educators restated the importance of **diversity** in U.S. schools and vowed to renew the fight to make it happen.

Children of different ethnic backgrounds share the same classroom as a result of desegregation.

Now Try This

Make a Difference at Your School

When asking for integration of the schools, Thurgood Marshall reminded the Supreme Court justices that African American and white children played together on the way to and from school. He asked what harm it would cause if they also went to school together. In making this point, Marshall suggested that if young people went to school together, they would remain friendly and helpful to each other.

What can you do to help people of different ethnicities and cultures in your school? Are some students being left out of social groups? Is anyone having difficulty with language? List the problems that you have observed. Interview students of other cultures to find out what they need in order to be happy at your school.

1. First, set a goal. You will need to focus on a problem that seems possible to solve. For example, you might decide to help students with language differences.
2. Next, make a plan. List the steps needed to solve the problem. Enlist the help of your classmates. Ask your teachers for suggestions. What else might help you make a plan?
3. Form a group and assign a task to each member of the group. If you want to deal with a language difference, the group might help a student learn English by holding practice conversations with him or her. One member of the group might pick a topic and another might make a list of English words that suit the topic. All members of the group should take part in the conversations.
4. You might want to turn the group into a club. Think of a name for the club. How will the name reflect the club's goal?

Thurgood Marshall on the cover of *Time* magazine

Glossary

aspiring *adj.* having an ambition for something; desiring earnestly; seeking.

discrimination *n.* the act of showing an unfair difference in treatment.

diversity *n.* variety.

doctrine *n.* what is taught as true by a church, nation, or group of persons; belief.

integration *n.* inclusion of people of all ethnic backgrounds on an equal basis in schools, parks, neighborhoods, and so on.

jeering *v.* laughing at rudely or unkindly; mocking; scoffing.

tactics *n.* ways to gain advantage or success; methods.